HEARTFULNESS: *TRANSFORMATION IN CHRIST*

HEARTFULNESS

Transformation in Christ

THOMAS KEATING

in Conversation with Betty Sue Flowers

WAYFARER BOOKS

SAN JUAN MOUNTAINS, COLORADO

WAYFARER BOOKS
SAN JUAN MOUNTAINS, COLORADO

All Rights Reserved
First Edition Published in 2024 by Wayfarer Books
Cover Design and Interior Design by Connor Wolfe
TRADE PAPERBACK 978-1-956368-97-0

10   9   8   7   6   5   4   3   2   1

SUPPORTING INDIGENOUS FUTURES
1% GIVEN BACK

God is All in All

That We May Be One

Open Mind, Open Heart

Manifesting God

Intimacy with God

Invitation to Love

The Human Condition

The Mystery of Christ

Awakenings

Reawakenings

Crisis of Faith, Crisis of Love

The Better Part

The Transformation of Suffering

The Heart of the World

Finding Grace at the Center

Spirituality, Contemplation & Transformation

The Daily Reader for Contemplative Living

Active Meditations for Contemplative Prayer

Betty Sue Flowers, PhD, is an Emeritus Professor of English at the University of Texas at Austin and the former Director of the Lyndon Baines Johnson Library and Museum. During her years at the University of Texas, she also served as Associate Dean of Graduate Studies and Director of the Plan II Honors Program. Her scholarly publications include a book entitled *Browning and the Modern Tradition*, and articles on Donald Barthelme, Adrienne Rich, Christina Rossetti, poetry therapy, writing, and other subjects.

Dr. Flowers also edited *Daughters and Fathers* with Lynda Boose, as well as four books in collaboration with Bill Moyers Joseph Campbell and the *Power of Myth; A World of Ideas; Healing and the Mind*; and *Genesis*. She edited the book and acted as a consultant to the 1988 documentary and nationally televised series, *The Power of Myth*, a series of interviews between Joseph Campbell and Bill Moyers.

Dr. Flowers was a host of the radio series "The Next 200 Years." Her ten-part television series, "Conversation with Betty Sue Flowers," aired on the Austin PBS affiliate, KLRU. She has served as a moderator for executive seminars at the Aspen Institute for Humanistic Studies, consultant for NASA, member of the Envisioning Network for General Motors, member of the vision team for the National Endowment for the Humanities (NEH), and Visiting Advisor to the Secretary of the Navy. Dr. Flowers was the editor of global scenarios for sustainable development and scenarios for the future of biotechnology, both sponsored by the World Business Council in Geneva.

Beloved Trappist monk Thomas Keating is best known as the one of the primary founders of the Centering Prayer movement, which made the contemplative dimension of Christianity accessible through a simple method of silent, still meditation. He is also known as the convener of the Snowmass Interreligious Conference, which helped birth the global Inter-spiritual movement.

Born in New York City in 1923, Keating's open invitation to people of all walks to embark on a spiritual journey, coupled with his emphasis on the oneness of all creation, made him a 20th-century harbinger of 21st-century ideals.

By promoting the practice of contemplative prayer through the non-profit Contemplative Outreach, Keating reached Christians within and beyond his Roman Catholic tradition, including 12 Step groups, incarcerated people, and people of all traditions and none—simultaneously connecting with contemplatives worldwide. Keating's work effectively expanded the common ground where spiritual diversity thrives in unity with what he called "the human family."

Keating often mused on the transformative power of silence, as revealed in one of his favorite sayings "Silence is God's first language. Everything else is a poor translation." Keating's love of silence infused his monastic life and spilled into the many books he wrote, including *Open Mind, Open Heart*, *Invitation to Love*, *Intimacy with God*, and *Divine Therapy and Addiction*.

Thomas Keating died on the 25th of October 2018 at the age of 95.

INTRODUCTION

A Reflection from Dr. Betty Sue Flowers

I first came across the work of Fr. Thomas through its effects on a class of students I was teaching in the Episcopal Seminary of the Southwest in Austin, Texas. As a former English professor who had taught world literature for many years, I was teaching classes in world religions using an academic rather than a spiritual or religious approach.

While many of the seminary students were exemplary, the last class I taught was quite special. From the first day, I noticed that the students in the class were—well, it's hard to describe, exactly. They were deeply *present*. There was a calm attentiveness and a kind of engaged joy. They were young, but noticeably mature. What accounted for this?

Halfway through the semester, a discussion about Buddhist meditation surfaced the fact that almost all of the students in the class were practitioners of a form of Christian meditation called "Centering Prayer" that they had learned from the works of Fr. Thomas Keating. Immediately after the class, I went to the Seminary bookstore and found *Open Mind, Open Heart: The Contemplative Dimension of the Gospel.*

And soon after that, I met Fr. Keating at a conference. His engaged and joyful presence confirmed, for me, that there was a gift in the practice of Centering Prayer that he taught and in his written works.

A few years later a student from that class, Mary Anne Best, who worked closely with Contemplative Outreach (an organization dedicated to making Centering Prayer and Fr. Thomas' works accessible), asked me to be involved in a series of taped interviews that we called *Heartfulness*.

From the beginning, the *Heartfulness* project was characterized by gratitude, good will, and humor. The core team—Mary Anne, Fr. Carl Arico, Gail Fitzpatrick-Hopler, and the video producer, Ray Mueller—dedicated a great deal of time and effort, overcoming numerous obstacles with a can-do spirit. Others helped us in this joyful task, including Mark and Ruth Dundon, the Fetzer Institute, the Circle of Friends, and other members of the Contemplative Outreach community who contributed to the support of the project.

Fr. Thomas himself was unfailingly patient and amazingly energetic. We talked for long stretches of time over a two-day period, and he never seemed to grow weary. He sustained that characteristic twinkle in his eye that makes you know that while the topics under discussion are deeply serious, in the end, the possibilities given in love for us as human beings are so wonderful that you cannot help but be grateful.

Our conversation ranged over many subjects, which made editing a challenge. Gradually, as we worked with the film, nine topics emerged as focal points: the pursuit of happiness, the human condition, Centering Prayer, sin, suffering, redemption, love and the Trinity, divine indwelling, and divine transformation.

The pursuit of happiness serves as a fundamental starting point because no matter what the faith (or lack of faith) or nationality or age or any other differentiator, humans desire happiness. Almost immediately in our conversation, Fr. Thomas shines a new light on the subject by saying that the desire for happiness "is itself the most certain sign of God's presence," and then offering both rational and empirical support for this claim.

It's worth pausing here for a minute to point out one of the powerful characteristics of Fr. Thomas as a spiritual teacher.

He speaks *with* authority—as someone who knows—but not *as* an authority. There is no "Believe this because I told you so" lurking within his words. With a kind smile—sometimes bordering on the mischievous, it seems to me—he offers a new possibility, which he eases into your mind and heart by appealing to common-sense reason and your own experience.

In this case, the new possibility is that God is at the center of the search for happiness. Implicit in so much of the misunderstanding that arises from commands such as "Take up your cross and follow me" is that to obey such a command means to give up the search for happiness. "Quit dancing and get grim!" But Fr. Thomas begins where we all begin—with ourselves as children, caught in the *human condition* in which we build a "false self" out of our need for security. This false self then leads us to search for happiness in all the wrong places—security, power, wealth, relationships. Fr. Thomas' analysis of this psychological process leads us both to understand and to have mercy on ourselves for our human erring.

In this context, repentance means to look in another direction for happiness. The new search for happiness is a spiritual journey "Everybody, by virtue of being born, is on the spiritual journey. There isn't any other choice." And this spiritual journey involves what Fr. Thomas calls "the Divine Therapy." It is here that the discipline of *Centering Prayer* offers the opportunity for listening and for opening up to "the True Self."

The elaboration of this therapeutic, or healing, process calls forth one of the many gifts Fr. Thomas' work offers the movement from a language of condemnation and judgment to a language of possibility, healing, and love. Such a language allows us to enfold psychological insights into our spiritual journey. Like all master teachers, Fr. Thomas uses examples and metaphors from our time to help us understand the timeless life of the Spirit.

This capacity to deepen our spiritual understanding through the inclusion of understanding from other domains, especially psychology, is one reason why Fr. Thomas' work is so illuminating. A thought such as the following combines both a psychological understanding of the self that serves to illuminate theology and an idea from theology that deepens psychology: "The psychological experience of a separate self sense is the root of all sin; get rid of that and there won't be any more serious sin."

The illumination that arises from the use of a full range of understanding in Fr. Thomas' teaching is especially helpful when it comes to understanding theological issues such as *sin* and *redemption*. We may have heard, for example, that the Greek word for "sin" comes from an archery term that means "missing the mark." Fr Thomas leads us to think more deeply about the implications of this. For example, consider the distinction between the practice necessary for eventually being a master archer—which involves failing over and over again—and the willful turning away from the target and shooting in the opposite direction. Similarly, Fr. Thomas' discussion about the journey of redemption is informed by analogies between the development of the soul and the process of biological evolution.

By the end of *Heartfulness*, Fr. Thomas has taken us deep into the difficult world of mysteries such as *love and the Trinity*, *divine indwelling*, and *divine transformation.* ("Christian service is not so much what we are doing for others as what Christ *in us* is doing for Christ *in them*.") With this dense material, the written version of *Heartfulness* is perhaps at its most helpful. Fr. Thomas makes a number of distinctions—for example, the distinction between *activity* ("in the form of effort") and *action* ("in the sense of accepting the goodness of God's presence"). Attempting to understand the significance of these distinctions to your own life can lead you to pause and ask: Where do I spend my time in activity rather than action? What difference would it make if I approached the spiritual journey as one of acceptance rather than effort? How can I best move from *activity* to *action*— without making that movement itself another form of activity?"

For me, one of the most moving discussions centers on *suffering*. In comparing the image of the serene Buddha with the image of Jesus on the Cross, Fr. Thomas says, "Our idea of death and of life is changed by looking at these two faces. Each has something incredibly profound to say about the Ultimate Reality and the ultimate meaning of suffering. The face of the

Buddha attests to the compassion of the Ultimate Reality. It says that everything, ultimately, is okay. Not only that, but that everything is delightful, perfect, good, beautiful, true, available. The face of Jesus is telling us that the Ultimate Reality totally identifies with the human condition at its most desperate, most abandoned, and most lonely point."

To live in this paradoxical understanding requires not just the brilliance of mind that we observe in Fr. Thomas, but also and more importantly the depth of heart that we also experience in his presence and that is available in all of us. Our hope is that experiencing *Heartfulness* will bless you as it has blessed us.

Betty Sue Flowers
AUTUMN 2009

FOREWORD

by Theodore Richards

I barely knew about Thomas Keating's work the first time I encountered him. I was a young and enthusiastic interfaith seminarian in New York City, and a classmate of mine told me he was offering a brief workshop on something called "Centering Prayer." So we took the train downtown to a church and sat in the small fellowship hall. I was an intense and passionate student at the time, eager to soak up whatever knowledge I could about the world's Wisdom Traditions. But that night, something else happened. After saying a few words, Father Keating, and the rest of us, just sat there. What I'd thought was going to be a lecture turned out to be something different—a shared exploration in stillness and quiet.

I wasn't unfamiliar with mindfulness practice. I'd explored the Buddhist and other forms of meditation. But the notion that there could be a *Christian* contemplative practice was a novelty for me. I appreciated some forms of Christian theology—the social gospel and liberation theology, for example—but these were about ideas, not praxis. They were about individual salvation, not collective transformation..

What I began to understand that day was that knowing something intellectually isn't the same as embodying it, feeling it, experiencing it. And when it comes to spirituality, there is a deeper knowing that comes from experiencing our connectivity to one another, to the divine, to the world. This is the beginning of mystical practice. In time, as my studies deepened, I came to see how Christianity, particularly since the Reformation, had repressed its contemplative and mystical roots. Father Keating was part of a small but growing movement to revive those practices.

One challenge, of course, is that everything about our world—the world of capitalism, of competition, of noise and busyness—seems to go against the contemplative life. As I was growing up, inactivity was discouraged. No. It was more than that. It was *shameful*. A person's value was connected to their busyness and productivity.

Father Keating challenges this value. What's more, he challenges the notion of individualism. The striving, busyness, and competition of the modern world are rooted in the basic, cosmological assumption that we encounter our world as individuals. Even our churches, focused as they are on individual salvation, fall into this trap. As Keating points out, it is this separate sense of self—individualism—that is the root of sin. I often wonder: in a world imbued with divinity, in which all is sacred, how could we even want to be "saved" while others are damned?

Contemplative practice points us in the direction of a spiritual location—not the literal location of heaven, but the spiritual location of the Kingdom of God—where the lines between you and me are blurred, where we are all in this together. This is not about an afterlife. Again, it defies our results-based culture. It is about now. Presence.

Father Keating calls on us to ask, over and over again: *What is happiness?* Like all of the most important questions, there's no simple or easy answer. But I can say that now, reading Father Keating's words twenty years later, in a different phase of life, I better understand the need for stillness. I better understand that we have created a civilization that cannot face up to the reality of suffering. We try to make the demons go away instead of facing them. This is the root of our addictions, collectively and individually. It is why we turn to our screens and our pills; it is why our addiction to consumption is destroying the planet.

Happiness does not mean the absence of suffering. That is an illusion, too, much like the individual self. Father Keating, like all the great mystics and contemplatives of any tradition, calls upon us to face the reality of our suffering. If we can slow down and experience, embody, the reality of our divinity and interconnectedness, we can get through it—not around it, but *through* it—because we are not alone.

Theodore Richards
WINTER 2024

"Heartfulness is more than an opening of the heart—it is a way of expressing the combined flow of openness of mind, heart, and being to support one's contemplative commitment…We hope that you will find support and guidance for your spiritual journey through *Heartfulness*, and we pray that the Spirit will reveal to you what is most necessary for your growth in the contemplative life at this time."

—Founding member and former President of Contemplative Outreach, Gail Fitzpatrick-Hopler

PART ONE

The Pursuit
of Happiness

DR. FLOWERS *I meet so many people who are yearning. They're hungry. Some know they're on a spiritual quest, that they're looking for God even if they don't call it "God." You've said that God is there already, as it were, waiting for them.*

FR. KEATING Happiness or the desire for happiness is itself the most certain sign of God's presence. No matter what you're looking for as a particular object of happiness, the very fact that you're looking, where does that come from? It's not something we inherit from the animals. They're looking for the immediate gratification of their instinctual needs. But humans have a sense they're looking for something more. We try to cover that up with special efforts to seek goods that are immediate or passing, but the fact that they never satisfy keeps reminding us that there is something more. That something more is the uneasy feeling that causes people, if they listen to that invitation, to go searching for a deeper meaning in life. As long as there is the desire for happiness—or the desire to get away from unhappiness—which is the same thing—this itself is the proof of God's existence and that he is within us.

FLOWERS *That adds another whole dimension to "life, liberty, and the pursuit of happiness." But the pursuit of happiness is usually taken to mean success in jobs, success in every other way.*

KEATING Yes. So what we understand by happiness is pretty important. Success in fame, fortune, and wealth—these tend to get drained of their excitement as we get older, especially in the midlife crisis, not to mention senility or the dying process.

The passage from life to death is really a very special time in most people's lives. Of its very nature it is a transformative period. The process of dying takes away the capacity for every kind of satisfaction that we might have hoped for. Everything recedes, and there is nothing left but you, whoever you are. The spiritual journey is really a deliberate anticipation of the passage of death, in which one freely and deliberately makes friends with this process and allows it to free one from the limitations of seeking happiness in self-centered pursuits. It also opens one's whole being to the possibilities that were unknown to us but which we've finally come to know in the dying process.

FLOWERS *But what if we don't want to wait until we die to find God or for God to find us? What if we want to make that connection before the end of life?*

KEATING If one makes any use of one's intelligence, I think that is what one would do! But the culture or peer group pressure or the thousands of years of making wrong decisions by our ancestors—all of these things weigh heavily upon us.

The human condition, it seems to me, adjusted to the simplest of language, should be taught in pre-school and continued in kindergarten and all the other grades all the way up to post-post-graduate school.

FLOWERS The human condition? What do you mean when you say "the human condition should be taught"?

KEATING By that I mean teaching how the false self comes into being, what its roots are, and what its consequences are, then going on to show how it is experienced in everyday life as a kind of vicious circle; how to deal with the frustrations of our emotional programs for happiness; how they get worse if we put more and more energy into them; and finally, where to go to find true happiness.

We are born with an innate desire for perfect happiness without knowing what it is, where it is, or how to get there. As infants, in order to survive, we seek the gratification of our instinctual needs for survival and security, power and control, and affection, esteem, and approval. As we grow up, these needs fossilize into demands that we try to impose on others and on society. We then find ourselves in competition with six and a half billion other people trying to do the same stupid thing. It can't possibly work, especially as we grow older. But the false self, based on the "programs" to find happiness in those first three emotional centers, never gives up. These programs, by the way, correspond to the first three chakras in the Hindu system, the energies of the "lower" self, which, when used merely selfishly, are comparable to the three temptations of Christ in the desert.

Some fulfillment of its instinctual needs is essential for the survival of an infant, but totally inappropriate for an adult. These desires or tendencies develop into a kind of center of gravity around which our thoughts, desires, and preoccupations tend to circle like planets around the sun. We envisage happiness as the maximum gratification of these desires. These emotional programs for happiness, together with the habits of mind and the cultural identifications that dominate our way of thinking, create the false self.

The net result of the false self is the sense of separation from God, from other people, and from all creation. We don't get what the essence of religions is trying to say because of the overlay of the preconceived ideas instilled in us in early childhood, before we had the use of reason, and thus we mistake the gratifications of our instinctual needs as happiness. The emotional programs for happiness just can't deliver, but we keep trying with bigger and better projects.

Society is dominated by sub-human motivation and the collectivity of false selves. These don't have the common good or the needs of others as their primary concern. Or, if they do, it's heavily influenced by selfish motivation.

Some people distinguish between a higher and lower ego. The ego is the self-identity that one develops with the help of the false self. With more maturity, the negative aspects of the false self may be somewhat reduced and the ego can become a positive influence.

But it is still very limited because its principal concern is itself—the *I am* of the false self. In the movie *Casablanca*, the hero, Rick, is a classic example of someone with a big ego. When Ilsa tries to persuade him to hand over the visas he possesses so she can escape Casablanca with her husband, she argues, "You helped out the rebels in Spain and you helped out in other causes." And he replies, "I'm the only cause I'm interested in." This is the Magna Carta of the false self. It is so unashamedly expressed by Rick that it hits you in the face, but we forget that this is exactly what we are doing most of the time.

The movement of openness to the True Self is obstructed by the habits and the deeply entrenched ways of thinking that are heavily defended and per-petuate the search for happiness in the wrong places.

Hence they lead to frustration, and the afflictive emotions that arise spontaneously are strong enough to ruin your health over time. If you are chronically angry, for example, you are pouring adrenaline into the bloodstream all the time, and eventually the arteries are going to give out. Whose fault is that? It's because we didn't look for happiness in the right place and put all our energy into projects that lead to human misery, lack of health, and the inability to relate to the Ultimate Reality, other people, and ourselves. It is a way of creating one's own personal hell. That is really what the bottom line is regarding the false self. We don't need any hell in the next life. It is right here for most people.

Repent means change the direction in which you're looking for happiness. That is the teaching of Jesus in the Gospels and the Sermon on the Mount. In other words, he is trying to undermine the energy we put into projects for happiness around the first three energy centers and the emotional programs for happiness that flow out of them. When frustrated, they give rise to the afflictive emotions of anger, grief, discouragement, shame, greed, lust, and avarice. The last three on that list are really compensatory aspects to get away from the pain of the frustration of what we have come to consider necessary for our happiness. Unless we are willing to go through a process of reducing them, we are not going to get too far in listening and relating to God in meditation and contemplative prayer.

FLOWERS *Then how do we get to the prayer, "Thy will be done," which really does enable us to see the help that is already there?*

KEATING By silence. By stopping, for a regular period of time, and as a discipline, the way we usually think. The only way to do that is by not thinking at all, at least deliberately, during a specific time, in order to open ourselves to the deeper dimension not only of our spiritual nature, with its intuitive capacity for knowing, but also of the spiritual will, which is the source of spiritual love within us. This opening leads to even deeper levels within us of the True Self and the Divine Indwelling, which is our true center.

FLOWERS *The True Self?*

KEATING The True Self is who God created us to be. It's who we are with our particular uniqueness as a manifestation of the Trinitarian life.

FLOWERS *And you say it already exists?*

KEATING It is if you exist. We are made in the image and likeness of God. It's not going to go away under any circumstances. We can try to change the direction in which we're looking for happiness, but we will not succeed without the grace of God. For a long time we may think that we will, and this will delay the process. Effort is designed not for success, but to find out that it doesn't work.

As soon as you let go of even a little bit, a crack occurs in our consciousness and some of the divine presence insinuates itself. The purpose of silence is to give an opportunity for the longing for God to break through the crust of the false self and our defense mechanisms, so that we can be motivated by the hunger and love to pursue the transformative process untiringly. It strengthens the soul to be willing to do almost anything, and it enhances its energy to pursue even difficult means in order to let go of whatever obstacles hinder us—hence, the willingness to let go of the things we most love, not as an end in itself, but as a means to free us from excessive attachment. God certainly wants us to love our family and all the pleasures of life. It is when we have been locked into the desire to make them substitutes for God that strong medication has to be applied. It is for that reason that I call this process "the Divine Therapy." Therapy is not always pleasant, but the therapist isn't out to kill us.

The Divine Therapist reveals himself to be a healer. What you are getting is an authentic, integrated view of yourself that is very realistic about your faults and over-dependencies. But you are less and less upset or humiliated by the knowledge of them. *Even though this is who I am, God loves me anyway.* It doesn't mean you don't want to improve, but you stop trying to succeed under your own steam. In other words, you wait for God to take away your faults rather than try to erase them yourself. Or, you pray that God will take them away. But if he doesn't, then you put up with them, just as Paul had to put up with his thorn in the flesh, although he begged to be free of it three times, a symbol of his desperation. God's response was, "My grace is sufficient for you." Not being over-anxious about getting over your faults empowers you to wait patiently for God to take them away.

What God wants is you—that is, the deep you, the you that is beyond the superficial self of your resume and the ego self of your emotional life—the *you* of the True Self, which is a manifestation of God's image in you. The spiritual journey is about finding out who you really are.

FLOWERS *And God would be there, it seems, at the bottom of things?*

KEATING I would think. In any case, this is what Jesus suggested in one of his famous wisdom sayings, "If you try to save your life"—meaning the life that you *think* is your life, based on the emotional programs for happiness and mistaken over-identifications with a particular group—"you will bring yourself to ruin. But anyone who brings himself to nothing, will find out who he is." It doesn't mean become nothing at all in the sense of annihilation, but become nothing in the sense of no attachment to anything. No objectifying of ourselves. *No thing* rather than nothing, is what is meant. Identifying with something prevents us from becoming what God is, which is everything.

In letting go of all our over-identifications, we start to realize who we really are—manifestations of the Eternal Word of God or of Christ. As Paul puts it, "I live now not I, but Christ lives in me." In other words, who I really am is becoming more and more the movement of the Spirit within me—not the *I am* of myself, but the great *I Am* of God.

From this perspective, it's easy to negotiate the entire spiritual journey because all you have to do is accept it. It is already happening. It has been communicated to us. It has been put into our hands. It has been put into our mouths. It has been poured into our hearts by the Holy Spirit. Are we willing to let God love us with this much unmerited gratuity?

PART TWO

The Human Condition

DR. FLOWERS *One of the things that I think is so helpful and even delightful about your writings on Centering Prayer is the way that you connect it to theories of the unconscious. Could you talk a little bit about the unconscious in relation to the spiritual journey and Centering Prayer?*

FR. KEATING The unconscious is a very significant aspect of the spiritual journey. As you know, it was discovered about a hundred and fifty plus years ago by Freud, and it has been pretty much accepted throughout the psychological community, whether they agree with some of his other ideas or not. The fact that there is an unconscious is certainly something that all religions have to take into account, especially if they present religion as a process or a spiritual journey with a series of stages.

Religion is not a brainwashing process, but rather a liberating process in which one freely accepts the journey and its consequences in our psychological awareness.

Depending on what is in the unconscious, we experience joy or distress when it comes to full awareness. How we handle that awareness and our attitude towards it is a crucial point for spiritual direction and for the proper negotiation of the spiritual journey.

We are told that as the child begins to separate from the mother and to develop a separate-self sense (after about eleven months or so), it begins to look upon the gratification of its instinctual needs for security, approval and affection, and power and control as the source of happiness. As it looks for the gratification of these programs, it seeks to avoid their frustration. Its ego develops as these programs for happiness fossilize into centers of gravity—call them "energy centers" for lack of a better term—in which their thoughts, desires, reflections, preoccupations, and behavior begin to circulate like planets around the sun. Thus any object, event, or person entering into that sphere of gravity is judged on the basis of whether it fulfills one of these emotional programs or hinders it, rather than on the objective value of this object, event, or person.

This is the beginning of a life of illusion, because we're looking at a world that has to conform to our desires, presuppositions, and expectations, and anything that doesn't fit in is unreal or unwanted.

As a result, we are not in contact with the objects themselves or with their objective value, if such they have. As this process continues to grow during the socialization period, from roughly four to eight, it becomes much more complex, because now we are relating with other developing egos plus important adults besides our parents. Now we have to deal with nurses, siblings, and teachers, as well as preschoolers and schoolmates.

By the time one hits conscious life, one is carrying a lot of baggage that is dynamite, depending on the situation. And as soon as an unpleasant experience explodes in your face, or mentally, or in your heart, off go—instantaneously and irrepressibly—feelings of grief, anger, humiliation, shame, discouragement, fear, and hatred, to mention only a few.

These reactions also get more complex. The more complex reactions Christian tradition calls the "capital sins," which are not personal sins but tendencies to trample on the rights and needs of others in pursuing one's own *I am* and one's own needs and wants.

These capital sins are pride, apathy, despair, avarice, envy, lust, and gluttony. Daily life consists in trying to deal with these afflictive emotions that go off with more or less severe consequences. And when these consequences become very painful, such as emotional trauma involving feelings like rejection, oppression, abandonment, loneliness, put-downs, and all the other hazards of growing up as a child, we repress some of them into the unconscious so that we don't have to feel them anymore. Their negative energy, however, lingers and is warehoused in the body, hidden from the victim, but often perfectly obvious to people who are close to us or live with us.

As soon as any feeling goes off, as Thomas Aquinas said in the 13th century, the body always is affected, a fact that is now reinforced by modern medicine. Just take anger as an example. Adrenaline is poured into the bloodstream when we are irritated. The commentaries of the imagination seem to be pre-recorded tapes. If you don't do something immediately to ward off the intensity of the feeling, the defenses go off, as does some appropriate commentary, such as, "How can they do this to me? I'm always treated badly. Nobody loves me." Or "I muffed it again." The clichés of our culture may exacerbate feelings like, "I must always get straight A's," or "What will mother say?" All of this stuff is sheer ego.

If occasionally we achieve what we want, we may fall into the other extreme, which is self-inflation, pride, and self-exultation, which are equally as harmful as depression, anger, and grief.

FLOWERS *It sounds like a kind of spiritual manic-depression—just going from one pole to the other.*

KEATING If it is extreme, you may actually be bipolar. The false self is neurotic in its tendencies, and it doesn't take much to establish it as a disease. Most people don't think of their false self or their ego as a disease, but it would be very helpful to them if they did.

Because then they would understand why they need the Divine Therapy.

FLOWERS *And maybe they would be up for it more. I mean, willing …*

KEATING Yes, have that motivation. That's why the Twelve Steps of A.A., are a step ahead of the rest of the population, in that those in recovery are aware of how unmanageable their lives actually are. Everybody's life is unmanageable. We just don't know it yet until it gets completely out of hand. Then we are forced to do something about it, or, in the case of alcoholism, we just die.

FLOWERS *But we're all addicted to ourselves, or our identities, it seems. Even more so than alcohol.*

KEATING Yes, and that is why recovery isn't the final cure of any illness because many people in recovery, as Bill W., founder of Alcoholics Anonymous observed, go into a depression after five or six years of sobriety.

Why? Perhaps the reason is that they haven't addressed the issue of emotional sobriety, which is the dismantling of the addictive process itself.

The addictive process is the false self. It almost certainly will develop into some kind of an addiction if we live long enough. The principal dynamic of the false self is to keep hiding from the pain of repressed material or repeated frustrations that are becoming intolerable.

The effectiveness of the Divine Therapy depends largely on one's commitment to consent to it. And one's commitment to consent depends in large part on how clearly one recognizes that one needs help. If you perceive that you have a serious illness, whether you get help or not is a matter of life and death. That is very clear in the addiction of alcohol. But since it is not that clear in the other addictions, or in the addictive process itself, people postpone, disregard, or hide from their guilt feelings and their painful emotions of grief and humiliation.

An addiction is the masterpiece of the false self in which you become so preoccupied with your addiction, from the point of view of time, tormenting desires, and preoccupations, that you haven't got any time to think about how much pain you have and are refusing to face. The healing consists in facing what you most dislike in yourself, which is causing the addiction in the first place. This service is what the Divine Therapy mercifully offers to provide. Jesus called himself a physician. I'm sure he would have included the psychiatric profession if it had existed in his day.

The result of bringing with us into daily life these unconscious desires that are then frustrated, causing us to over-react, is not because of the situation, but because of the baggage. The present problem reminds us of this, and then our internal commentaries raise the initial distress to ever greater levels of intensity. If it is anger, we move from irritation to anger,

anger to rage, and then rage to temporary insanity. By the time we reach that last stage, we obviously wind up in an emotional binge, which may last for several hours, or the whole day, or for a week, and sometimes, for some people, the rest of their lives.

This is the spiritual journey in reverse. Or rather, the spiritual journey going in the opposite direction at top speed. It is based on the emotional illness called the "false self," which, in turn, is based on not knowing where true happiness is to be found. Hence, it is almost inevitable—so inevitable that it has come to be called, in the Christian tradition, the consequences of original sin. The common patrimony of humanity is the result of our first parents having rejected God in the Judeo-Christian scheme of things, but which, from a scientific point of view, could also be looked at as a failure to evolve from lower forms of life.

As human beings we start out in life with this heavy strike against us, namely, the misunderstaning that the gratification of our emotional programs for happiness *is* happiness or can lead to happiness. In pursuing emotional programs for happiness that can't possibly work, you are solidifying the basis of a life of human misery. You will be constantly frustrated in trying to find happiness in the gratification of one of these programs, or in over-identifying with false belief systems that have been interiorized as a result of religious, patriotic, ethnic, or family enculturation. There are values in every culture, but they are not absolutes.

Finding out how to raise the human condition to an awareness of this situation, with its urgency and vast ramifications, and how to reduce distractions that prevent us from exposing ourselves fully to the reality of our unconscious are crucial for the positive change society depends on. No amount of politics or discussion is going to change society for the better until enough people change themselves, so that societies around the world are not pouring more negative energy into the same old cesspool. There is no way we can separate ourselves from being part of this melodrama.

Actually, one feels more and more immersed in the human situation as one is liberated from the false self.

The contemplative journey is the most responsible of all responses to God because so much depends on it—the future of humanity, the healing of the wounds of humanity, our own deepest healing. It's not just a method of meditation or a practice to find personal peace. It's basically a total acceptance of the human condition in all its ramifications, including its desperate woundedness, all of which is symbolized in the Agony in the Garden of Gethsemane and the cup that Jesus was asked to drink. No merely human person could possibly drink to the dregs the capacity for human brutality and evil that humans are capable of. At the same time, what makes it even more tragic is that humans are fully capable of becoming God, not in the fullest sense of the term, but in a very real way, where the light, life, and love of God are pouring through them, channeling a source of healing, compassion, and reconciliation wherever they go and whatever they do. They are rooted in the divine compassion and mercy, and are manifesting, not the false self anymore, nor the emotional junk in the unconscious, but the pure light of the image and *likeness* of God within them, which is the assimilation of the mind and heart of Christ in everyday life.

FLOWERS *Could you talk a little bit about the unconscious in relation to the spiritual journey and Centering Prayer?*

KEATING The unconscious is a very significant aspect of the spiritual journey. As you know, it was discovered about a hundred and fifty plus years ago by Freud, and it has been pretty much accepted throughout the psychological community, whether they agree with some of his other ideas or not. The fact that there is an unconscious is certainly something that all religions have to take into account, especially if they present religion as a process or a spiritual journey with a series of stages.

Religion is not a brainwashing process, but rather a liberating process in which one freely accepts the journey and its consequences in our psychological awareness.

Depending on what is in the unconscious, we experience joy or distress when it comes to full awareness. How we handle that awareness and our attitude towards it is a crucial point for spiritual direction and for the proper negotiation of the spiritual journey.

PART THREE

Centering Prayer

DR. FLOWERS *Many people get confused when they think about prayer. They think it means talking to God all the time. But Centering Prayer seems to be different. Centering Prayer seems to be mainly concerned with silence, which you say is the language of God. For someone for whom that's a strange notion, or for someone who's never come across this in Christianity and thinks, "Well, is this some sort of New Age concept out of Eastern meditation?"—how could this be clarified?*

FR. KEATING Centering Prayer came out of a desire to renew, recover, and reclaim the Christian contemplative tradition. It could just as well be called "contemplative prayer." It doesn't have to be called "Centering Prayer." The problem at the time Centering Prayer appeared was that "contemplation" had taken on several different meanings, including opposing meanings. Sometimes it referred to looking at something, like contemplating a tree or a picture, or mentally contemplating some memory, or projecting a plan for the future. The classical meaning of contemplation, which I believe comes out of Matthew 6:6, and which Jesus calls "prayer in secret," is about a deepening relationship that involves the intention to converse with God, to open and consent to God's presence. To converse with God presupposes a willingness to listen to God.

Listening is an act of silence. You cannot hear what somebody else is saying if you are talking all the time. Prayer as relationship emerges as the essence of prayer, which can then be expressed in many different ways. The classic ways of praying are petition, which is asking for things; adoration, which is responding to God's transcendence and goodness; and gratitude, which is responding to the good things we receive from God or the good things we hear about in scripture. It may express trust or love in the mystery that is laid before us in scripture, nature, or in some other way. Thus, praying is any of these dispositions or interior acts. But prayer itself might best be reserved for one's relationship with God, based on one's present level of communion or at-ease-ness with God in ordinary life. If we are scared to death of God, then we have a relationship to God, but it's not a very appealing one. It tends to make us want to run away, or to postpone the encounter to another time

In Jesus' wisdom saying in Matthew 6:6 he gives a formula of prayer that is also a formula for cultivating interior silence. The first step is to enter our inner room. It is sometimes translated "private room," but most people didn't have a private room in those days. The Desert Fathers and Mothers interpreted this saying to refer to the spiritual level of our being. The invitation that Jesus extends is to enter our inner room, symbol of the spiritual level of our being, which is the level of intuition and the spiritual will, the realm of true choice.

FLOWERS *So, if I want to enter into this relationship, to pursue this path, what do I do? I know it's a "not doing," but how do I do "not doing"?*

KEATING First of all, there are a lot of things you have to do in the way of bringing your life on the conscious level into some accord with your aspirations. You have to let go of things that are obviously serious obstacles and to cultivate habits of mind and heart and behavior that are conducive to this listening process and exchange.

FLOWERS *So, in a way, what you're saying about Centering Prayer is that it isn't like some of these other things on the market that offer you rest, relaxation, happiness, peace. You've described it as a series of humiliations of the false self, which doesn't sound like a very pleasant experience. And then people talk about things like the "dark night of the soul." And so, really, Centering Prayer seems to be about a journey that isn't just the kind of superficial happiness that you might get from having a restful period twice a day.*

KEATING It is not a magic carpet to bliss, that's for sure. It's a transformative process that involves, to put it bluntly, the death of the false self.

This shouldn't be a surprise to Christians, because in Baptism, they've already agreed to do this, if they were conscious at the time. The symbolism of the baptismal rite involves descent into the water, or more exactly, into the purification that is one of the symbols of water in scripture, and then the emersion out of the water. Just immersion would not do it. You don't emerge from nothing, you emerge from something. What we emerge from in the baptismal pool is the attachment to the sinful and self-centered projects of life that are rooted in the emotional programs for happiness and excessive dependence on groups to which we belong. By that I mean that one is prepared not to think about one's own individuality, conscience, or integrity, but to subject all these things to the approval of the group in order to be accepted. This is not a healthy attitude, and Jesus attacked it strongly in the wisdom saying "Unless you give up your family and children and wife and property, and your inmost self, for my sake, you can't be my disciple." The life that was built up around those instinctual needs for happiness has to go.

FLOWERS *Saying goodbye seems to be really key to the whole process.*

KEATING Little by little we enter into prayer without any other intention except to consent. Consent becomes surrender. And surrender becomes total receptivity as this process evolves. And total receptivity is effortless. It has nothing to do with attaining something, or getting anything, or the desire for enlightenment, peace, or spiritual experience. Such desires are still ego, however devoutly masked. So, no thinking, no reflecting, no expectations, no words.

Everything is impermanent, which is another way of saying everything is changing. That is the nature of reality. Or to put it another way, God is not a noun, not an object. A better metaphor would be a verb. That is, he is always happening. Hence the thing that doesn't change about God is that he is always changing.

The discipline of Centering Prayer gradually adapts us to this mystery of the Ultimate Reality by enabling us to change and to let go of everything that prevents us from doing so. As a penitential people, our chief job is to keep letting go of our attachments as we perceive them, especially those that we feel are opposed to love. One of these obviously would be an unwillingness to forgive. Another would be a tendency to judge others harshly, including ourselves.

The less we think of ourselves, the better this process goes, as well as faster. The formula that Jesus gave us in Matthew 6:6, on which Centering Prayer is based, is a kind of cascading movement into deeper levels of silence in which we first deliberately let go of the external tumult of the world and all our immediate anxieties and concerns and turn them over to God for the twenty minutes to a half an hour we agree to spend in Centering Prayer.

It is not a question of doing something but of being with God intentionally for these twenty minutes. When this is challenged by the usual flow of thoughts, which are inevitable, we simply, quietly, without being annoyed or distressed, return to our original intention by some symbol. The latter has no inherent value in itself, but is simply a way of renewing our atten- tiveness to the general loving presence that we are calling God.

As a practical disposition, when one sits down in Centering Prayer, this is a time to have no judgment about anything at all—no judgment about the period of prayer and its psychological content, still less about what's happening in the world, and still less about judging other people or evaluating circumstances. All judgment, indeed all reflection, is not appropriate during the time of Centering Prayer, which is a time of sharing one's pure being with God. It is not time for action. It is a time of complete receptivity, a time for consenting to whatever is happening at this present moment. It is an exercise of being with God in the present moment.

In Centering Prayer, it is what you don't do that counts most. The term "thoughts" refers to any perception whatsoever during the time of prayer. Since thoughts are inevitable, given the fact that the imagination is a perpetual motion faculty, consent means to let what happens happen. One does not resist the thoughts that come down the stream of consciousness. Nor does one hang onto them, which would be getting engaged with them. Nor does one react emotionally to them, or to the state of having them in the first place. In other words, it is just sitting down and being still. That is to say, being quiet on every level. Although it is just for a limited time, it is sufficiently powerful to undermine the thought patterns of the false self around the energy centers and over-identification with our group.

FLOWERS *How can you help your capacity to receive?*

KEATING By giving up the false self. That is what is busy doing something all the time. And what it's doing is useless. By discontinuing that activity, one has a great deal of time for constructive activity, such as service of others, and can rest even in the midst of action.

> **FLOWERS** *It seems to me that, paradoxical though it sounds, people who are on this journey, who succeed to some extent in getting rid of this false self, appear more truly unique. They appear to be more individual than people who are hard at work creating their own individuality. A real uniqueness shows through. It makes them extremely attractive to other people, who want to be around that beauty of the unique.*

KEATING All I could say to that is, what are you waiting for? All you have to do is stop being who you think you are, and you couldn't be more delightful! Because there's nothing more beautiful than the uniqueness that God has created in us. It's just buried like a diamond underneath a pile of garbage. That is not God's fault, but the misuse of our freedom and the imposition on us of all the negative forces in the environment and our social milieu.

It is a job to climb out of those influences. But all the work is in letting go of those influences and not reinforcing them. You don't have to create the beauty—you've got the beauty. You don't have to create the freedom—you've got it. You don't have to create the image of God in you—you have it. You don't have to win over God's love—you have more than you know what to do with. You don't have to become more beautiful—because nothing could be more beautiful than your own, particular uniqueness.

PART FOUR

Sin

DR. FLOWERS *What is sin?*

FR. KEATING First of all, its source, it seems to me, is the separate-self sense. Once we have established that, we can see that the source of moral evil, whether it is social or personal, is the radical sense of separation from God. And not experiencing who God is as loving Father, as Jesus teaches.

FLOWERS *And having no hope of such an experience?*

KEATING Right.

FLOWERS *That is despair.*

KEATING Despair is the ultimate sin. But aside from that, there is the deliberate rejection or indifference to the needs and rights of others and preferring our own self-interest to others' real or even desperate needs, because we are the only cause we are interested in—that is, furthering our self-centered goals—fame, wealth, success, pleasure—whatever the culture presents as symbols of security, power, affection, and esteem.

The psychological experience of a separate-self sense is the root of all sin. Get rid of that and there won't be any more serious sin. It is the anxiety, the sense of separation, loneliness, or alienation—and all these negative feelings that flow from them—that are really the inspiration of seeking what we imagine as happiness, wherever it can be found, without being concerned about the consequences.

"Sin" actually has a very interesting etymological history. It comes from a Greek word meaning "to miss the mark," a term from the art of archery. What does missing the mark actually involve? It presupposes a target and the center of the target, which is called the bullseye. A bow is the means by which the archer tries to launch an arrow into the center of the target. The purpose of the art of archery is to hit the target every time, or to get as close to doing so as possible.

This accomplishment does not happen easily or soon for those who are apprenticing to this art. The chances of hitting the bullseye with the first shot are practically nil. Is this surprising? Nobody expects you to hit the bullseye in the beginning. Only by mastering the subtlety of the discipline can you put the arrow into the bullseye or come anywhere near it.

The most successful archers have learned to develop first of all their tools, how to use their bow and arrow, so that through long and frequent practice, which involves missing the mark most of the time, they develop a sense of the space, time, distance, wind, and other factors. Then the arrow has a good chance of striking the bullseye.

What would be the proper response to missing the bullseye if you were an apprentice? Obviously, try again.

FLOWERS *"If at first you don't succeed, try, try again."*

KEATING That is all you have to do.

So to lament the fact that one doesn't hit the bullseye at the first shot is ridiculous. It is a skill to be learned gradually, and it is learned by adjusting the body, the nerves, the muscles, and the tension of the string and its relation to the arrow. When everything has been perfectly attuned through practice and a sense of physical and even spiritual poise, the expert archer will hit the bullseye every time without effort. That level of skill can't be achieved by effort. The right effort goes into the preparation and the skills to be attained. Once they are attained, the archer scarcely has to look at the bullseye. He has a feel for the practice. One look at the target and the distance, and he knows the exact moment in which to let the arrow fly. It is the letting go under those circumstances and with the right timing that carries the arrow unerringly to the bullseye.

FLOWERS *The letting go under the circumstances of having practiced.*

KEATING Yes. In other words, to allow the divine energy to work through us, through the preparation that has been done through many, many failures. We are not relying on our own skill to do this, but on becoming an instrument at one with the divine action that is manifesting in this particular skill. Only now the skill is in the service of others and responding to the events of life, whether eating, sleeping, drinking, walking, working, thinking, talking, playing. In the spiritual journey, purity of intention and the love of God enable us to hit the target in each of our daily activities, effortlessly.

> **FLOWERS** *Is it possible to have gained the expertise of the expert archer, hitting the bullseye every time with ease, in such a way that the outside world sees the fruits of the Spirit in your life, and yet on the inner dimension to have a sense of dryness, desert, or aridity?*

KEATING The painful feeling doesn't really matter because it is only a thought, and we are not our thoughts. We just have an endless stream of them. People normally see the exercise of the skill and admire that. However, it may be so hidden in the ordinariness of daily life that nobody takes notice of it. It depends on the level of perceptivity of those who are watching and who might have some appreciation of what must have gone into an action that makes such a witness to the divine presence possible.

> **FLOWERS** *I know some people whom I would consider very holy, who sometimes talk about a dryness, or a period of their lives when they don't feel the consolation of God. Then it is pure faith that they are in.*

KEATING Pure faith is part of the skill in applying the metaphor of the art of archery to the spiritual life, and without that, you won't hit the mark. Both love and trust have to be pure. That is to say, pure of the motives that were hidden in the unconscious but have now become conscious and deliberately let go of in the course of the transformative process, both in prayer and in everyday life. In other words, it is letting go at the right moment, the right place, and in the right way. Once the preparation has been made, then the accomplishment is not really attributable to the archer, but rather to the skill of the trainer, which in this case is the Holy Spirit. Or, to quote God's words to Saint Paul, "My strength is made perfect in weakness." It is not our skill that is the reason we hit the bullseye, but our willingness to be an instrument of God and to fulfill the necessary conditions physically and mentally for this to happen.

Now it so happens that human behavior, especially divine human behavior, is even more of a skill than the art of archery, or any other art. They are paradigms, or metaphors, of the skill of just being present to what is and being content with what is without wanting to change it, but willing to change it if such is the divine inspiration. It is life under the guidance or the discipline of the Holy Spirit, manifesting divine love in every situation.

Without love there is no virtue. There is only apparent virtue. Divine love is the center of a circle in which the apparent opposite virtues are present, such as mercy and justice, gentleness and firmness, humility and trust.

How do you know when to practice mercy, and when justice? You don't. But love teaches you how to reconcile the opposites so that what you do hits the target instead of missing it.

> **FLOWERS** *And it's not a learning once and for all. It is a learning in the moment. It's not something you learn to practice. It's the learning that occurs in the center of the moment.*

KEATING The invitation of the Gospel is to give up damaging activity. In the metaphor of archery, if you take a pot shot at the bullseye and miss, that is one way of missing the mark. But if you turn around and shoot in the opposite direction, with the intention of never hitting the bullseye, this is a wholly different attitude. You will reap the consequences, one of which is, you do not ever hit the bullseye. Whose fault is that? To blame that failure on God is ridiculous. If we chose to do it, we have to accept the consequences of our choice.

We have a genuine level of freedom, however narrow the window may be because of psychological factors that diminish freedom in situations of passion. That is why premeditated murder is much more serious than killing someone out of passion. The same goes for all other forms of human misbehavior where there are excusing circumstances, where there is a limited amount of understanding of where the evil involved is, or where the consequences, responsibility, and accountability of our actions are obviously much less, or perhaps may not exist at all, as in the case of neurotic activity and still more in the case of mental disease.

FLOWERS *Then how are we to understand Judgment Day in that context?*

KEATING There is no doubt that scripture speaks of this last day and an ultimate judgment. Whatever that means as a social event, our own last judgment is our own death. That is the last day as far as we are concerned. For all practical purposes, our death is the judgment. But who judges? Jesus says he doesn't judge. And the Father says he doesn't judge. So who is left? You and I. So when we shed the body and the brain, with all its predispositions and inclinations to justify or rationalize, then perhaps for the first time our spiritual will is actually empowered to make a decision that is totally free.

When all of our defenses, the body, and the ways that we have known reality have fallen away, what is left is just the divine light, and that light, which is the image of God in us, sees very clearly what our state of soul is and where we should go. We don't need anybody's help. We see much more clearly than we've ever seen, exactly what our state of soul is. But we also will see those aspects that have marred or dimmed our uniqueness, and what you do with this is between you and God. There is no need for discussion.

FLOWERS *That's the life review that people talk about?*

KEATING Yes. Actually, God will be on your side, because the judgment is about mercy.

PART FIVE

Suffering

DR. FLOWERS *I think suffering is such a problem in Christianity and for people in general.*

FR. KEATING It is a subject that is central to all of the religious belief systems, or to people with no belief system, because it is a major part of living. There are two very striking symbols of happiness achieved in this world through spiritual attainment. They express two different ways of experiencing suffering that, taken together, might help to explain the statement by many mystics that suffering is the shortest and surest path to wisdom.

In Buddhism the symbol of spiritual attainment is called "nirvana," a state that the Buddhists consider perfect happiness. This interior state is symbolized by the smile of the Buddha. That smile expresses perfect equanimity, serenity that has risen above every conflict and all inner and outer suffering, and seems to be looking inwardly at the Ultimate Reality with a delight that is not exuberant, but absolutely mature.

FLOWERS *It's a smile not in reaction to something that's happened. It seems to come from within.*

KEATING It is almost the epitome of the Buddhist approach, which is to recognize suffering as an essential part of life, but also to overcome all suffering. The face of the Buddha with its beautiful and very delicate smile is the symbol that all suffering has been overcome. At the same time, it is the symbol of utmost compassion, which is at one with all suffering without experiencing the pain. In other words, it expresses an inner state where suffering has been transcended.

> **FLOWERS** *In his poem "Lapis Lazuli," Yeats has a beautiful image of Chinese wise men on a mountainside, looking down at all the tragedy, but calling for music. He says, ". . . their ancient glittering eyes were gay." They see the tragic scene, but they see it from a distance, from a certain perspective.*

KEATING Yes, and that perspective is, at least in part, complete detachment—oneness and detachment at the same time. It is an incomparable image of the essence of Buddhist practice and faith.

Let's look at another image: the face of Jesus on the cross. This is a face that is the reverse of equanimity. It is the face of a man who is dying of thirst, bloodied by blows all over his body, wearing a crown of thorns on his head, and whose lips utter a cry of abandonment.

The nature of crucifixion in those days was especially harsh since people usually suffocated to death as they struggled to breathe in spite of the excruciating pain that any movement in their arms or legs or bodies was sure to cause.

We have here two images that seem to be almost reversed. And so the question inevitably emerges: what is the ultimate meaning of suffering? Or what experience of suffering do these two faces represent that seem so opposite, but which epitomize the spiritual teaching of each of these two great wisdom teachers?

Buddha's face is one of exquisite serenity, peace, tranquility, transcending all suffering while remaining united to everyone who is suffering. There is no effort to change anything. There is simply total acceptance of what is. And the smile suggests that everything, just as it is, is perfect.

In the face of Jesus on the cross we see an altogether different expression. Jesus in his passion and death, according to Saint Paul, is identified with everybody's suffering. He physically, mentally, and spiritually epitomizes the most intense kind of suffering imaginable. His is just the reverse of the Buddha's external expression of equanimity and transcendence of all suffering. Jesus is immersed in it, overwhelmed by it, totally powerless to control it or reduce it. And yet he expresses in his own way the same disposition of total acceptance of what is

"Father, into your hands I commend my spirit." He accepts out of incomparable love the cruelest of deaths and the rejection on the social level of everything he stood for and taught.

The question naturally arises: which is the most exact portrait of the meaning of suffering? Is it the face of the Buddha, transcending all suffering? Or is it the face of Jesus, utterly immersed in it? They are such striking contradictions that they force us to open ourselves to the possibility that both are perfect expressions of reality. Since they contradict each other, the ultimate meaning of suffering must transcend both.

The teaching that is being expressed by these two images is incomparable. Suffering, by general consent, is an inevitable and unavoidable part of life.

It is life. Suffering and death are not the opposite of living, but are part of what human life actually is. Our idea of death and of life is changed by looking at these two faces. Each has something incredibly profound to say about the Ultimate Reality and the ultimate meaning of suffering.

FLOWERS *And what do they have to say? If you imagine looking at those two faces, what is it that they say to you?*

KEATING We each have to answer that question for ourselves. The face of the Buddha attests to the compassion of the Ultimate Reality. It says that everything ultimately is okay. Not only that, but that everything is delightful, perfect, good, beautiful, true, available.

The face of Jesus is telling us that the Ultimate Reality totally identifies with the human condition at its most desperate, most abandoned, and most lonely point. Jesus' passion and death is the result, in Christian terms, of his identification with the human condition and of alienation from God, which is the result of the deliberate rejection of God on whatever level and in whatever degree one has deliberately sinned. In Jesus on the cross we are looking at the consequences of sin in its naked reality, intensity, and horror. What we are looking at is our own inner sense of alienation visibly expressed. The consequences of rejecting God are unbearable loneliness and the hellishness that is the natural consequence of rejecting God and of rejecting all that is good in others, in creation, and in oneself. It represents what self-hatred looks like in the concrete.

FLOWERS *Self-hatred?*

KEATING Self-hatred is also the hatred of God, because God and ourselves are united. What we are looking at in Jesus' suffering and death is the reverse image of the Buddha and his experience of unfathomable peace. The True Self is the Ultimate Reality manifesting in a human being. In Jesus on the cross, it is sin manifesting as a human being, and God's reaction to it, which is to identify with it, and in identifying with it at every level, even to its very depths, to transmit a love that is so intense that it transforms sin itself into the pure love of God. But this love is hidden by the enormity of the reality of identification with sin and its consequences that may not be quite complete, even in Jesus' death.

The Apostles' Creed, which contains the fundamental doctrines that Christians adhere to, says that he then "descended into hell." What is so striking here is that Christ has embraced not only his own sufferings but everyone else's and made them his own. He not only identifies with them out of boundless compassion; he is "made sin," as Paul says, taking the consequences into himself and penetrating all suffering with a divine meaning that manifests the inner nature of God, which is infinite self-giving, the sacrifice of all that one is.

> **FLOWERS** *Many people think of suffering as a kind of punishment, and so, like Job, they ask, "God, why is this happening to me?" They feel that if they could only figure out why, they could do something about it, and the suffering would cease. Is that a mistake?*

KEATING Some suffering is inevitable. It goes with disasters of a natural kind that we have no control over, including asteroids that might pop down on the earth, as seems to have happened in past millennia.

The whole of creation and life itself emerge out of chaos and out of the enormous collisions of galaxies in outer space. Protein molecules and other elements necessary for life are only possible when galaxies crash together and reach a certain temperature in which new elements can be formed. The message of creation is that out of physical or natural disasters on the galactic level come the conditions out of which more developed forms of existence and especially life can eventually emerge.

A prime mistake we all tend to make is attributing to God our own very limited thoughts and perspectives about suffering, complaining, "How can God do this to me? I'm serving him, and you'd think he'd give me some help." Even Paul had this problem. He was shipwrecked, beaten up, rejected by his people, and stoned, even though he preached the Gospel tirelessly everywhere. You might think, why didn't God help him out? Instead, Paul got thrown into prison and had his head cut off. Persecution or opposition is a sign of a special calling from God and not a sign that God doesn't love you. Rather it is a sign that God is guiding you into the dynamics of genuine transformation that you see in nature. The transformation of lower forms of life is the only way evolution moves on to higher forms of life. It is doubtful that that rhythm is going to change.

It is important for Christians to realize there really is no punishment in God. This is a projection of our thinking onto God. And even the threats that you find in the New and Old Testaments may be the only way to get people to re-think their negative or damaging behaviors. But all divine threats are reversible.

The Divine Therapy is relentless in its zeal to heal our wounds. It arranges circumstances in our lives—however horrendous, in our opinion—that enable us to look deeper into our unconscious and to be more vulnerable to its contents, without being the least bit discouraged or falling into despair—rather, loving the honesty, truth, authenticity, and integrity of being exactly who God wants us to be in the present moment and responding accordingly. One then becomes a channel of divine grace rather than a paragon of merely human virtue.

PART SIX

Redemption

FR. KEATING Thomas Aquinas teaches that God could have forgiven man's sin, or more exactly, the sin of Adam and Eve, with its consequences for the rest of the human race, by a simple act of the divine will. God did not have to require the suffering and death of his Son. This suggests that the primary motive for Christ's Incarnation and redemptive work is to manifest the full extent of the goodness of God by an act that revealed the overflowing generosity of God's love for us. The humility of God moved Him to identify with the reality of human suffering and death in the person of his incarnate Son. Thus, a corner of the veil that conceals the inmost nature of the Ultimate Reality was lifted.

If God's beloved Son, at the Father's request, identifies with the human condition and sin, what does that say about the divine relationship of Father and Son in the Trinity? It reveals that God is eternally sacrificing what he loves most for our sake. It also involves, on the part of Jesus, the realization that in accepting the physical, psychological, and spiritual consequences of sin, he is alienating himself from the Father's infinite love. If his identification with us is truly real, Jesus must endure a sense of being rejected by God since the sense of alienation is the very essence of deliberate sin. Is this only a symbolic gesture? Or is this a real rejection? Jesus cries out as he nears death, "My God, my God, why have you forsaken me?" In other words, "How could you do this to me, your beloved Son?" The only response is silence. By Jesus consenting to be made sin, the Father's boundless love, while seeming to be rejected, is revealed in the most sublime way.

Redemption through Jesus' suffering and death is not limited to the work of saving us from the consequences of sin. That liberating action, according to scripture, is the necessary condition in order for the human race to be transformed into God, and it is the latter that is the ultimate purpose of Jesus' sacrifice.

Through his passion, death, and resurrection, Jesus heals the human family of the whole gamut of its limitation and failures, inviting us into participation in the divine life in the fullest degree that we can possibly receive.

The immense importance of Christ's redeeming work remains. The question is: what does the term "redemption" actually mean? What motive is behind the decision of the Father to ask Christ, his Beloved Son, to become sin, that is, to become the opposite of all that the Father is? Jesus reveals by his actions the humility of the Father who is prepared to go to any length in order to communicate the divine life in all its fullness to the human family, insofar as we are capable of receiving it.

There is a further consideration. The reason that Jesus consented to be made sin for our sakes is because his great love for the Father impelled him to manifest, in the most visible and fully human way, the extraordinary love that he had for the Father. It led him to reveal its magnitude by a sacrifice that involved enormous human and even divine suffering. He gave up being God in his Incarnation in order to become one with us, enabling us to become the children of God by participating in the divine life. The work of redemption is not so much the paying of an enormous price to buy back us slaves of sin as it is a tremendous affirmation of God's compassion for the human family in our present evolutionary predicament, as we transition from animal to rational consciousness, the gate to all the higher stages of consciousness.

Thus, the fall from grace of our first parents is not the only way to explain the human condition. It can be explained as a lack of evolutionary development from the lower forms of life. Perhaps both perspectives contribute to the actual reality. In any case, Jesus' life and death have given the human family a profound thrust in the direction of divine transformation. As long as our spiritual evolution as human beings has not matured to a certain point, our idea of God and our relationship to other people and to ourselves will continue to regress to sub-human, or animal, levels of behavior, especially in times of conflict.

Our vocation is to move beyond these lower levels and to contribute to the building up of the Mystical Body of Christ, in which the full extent of the human potential is gradually being manifested. Can that transformation be achieved in this world? The Christian mystics believe that it can. In their view, redemption, in the sense of transformation into the divine way of being human, is available in this life to everyone.

Just how large a proportion of humanity will be able to access this divine way of being human we don't know. But we may reasonably raise the question whether the theological opinion of redemption as payment for sin is by itself an adequate way to present the truth of who the Father is. And revealing who the Father is seems to be the major concern and purpose of Jesus' life and teaching.

FLOWERS *It is a revelation that still hasn't been fully understood.*

KEATING Yes, and I don't think it will until enough people have negotiated the transformative process and are able to interiorize the spiritual implications and ultimate significance of Christ's sacrifice. Scripture provides examples of persons who actually had that insight—for instance, Mary of Bethany, anointing Jesus at Simon the leper's house. By breaking an alabaster jar of very expensive perfume over the whole body of Jesus and filling the house with the gorgeous scent, she seems to have intuited what Jesus was about to do on the cross. The authorities were set on killing him. What her lavish gesture symbolized was the deepest meaning of Jesus' passion and death. The body of Christ is the jar containing the most precious perfume of all time, namely, the Holy Spirit. It was about to be broken open so that the Holy Spirit could be poured out over the whole of humanity—past, present, and to come—with boundless generosity. Until that body had been broken on the cross, the full extent of the gift of God in Christ and its transforming possibilities for the human race could not be known or remotely foreseen.

Jesus in his passion and death walked away from the greatest love there is out of a still greater love for the Father, who willed to transform the entire human family. Transformation in Christ—deification—is thus the full meaning of the redemption.

PART SEVEN

Love and
the Trinity

DR. FLOWERS *You say so often in your work that God is a loving God and that his relationship to us is one of a lover. What distinguishes a lover's relationship to God from any other? And what about the paradox that increasing the capacity to love in this Christian path also increases the capacity to suffer?*

FR. KEATING Yes, but it is not the same kind of suffering as occurs in the beginning, because one sees a certain value in suffering and the path to divine wisdom. There is something about the nature of God in which sacrifice is primary. From this perspective sacrifice is the meaning of the universe.

FLOWERS *Sacrifice?*

KEATING Sacrifice is the total gift of oneself or all that one is. This goes on eternally in the relationships within the Trinity, where sacrifice is delightful.

Divine goodness gives itself away infinitely, totally, and without ceasing. Of course, anything we say about the Trinity can only point to certain aspects, all of which are beyond any concept and can only be fully experienced in the next life. Divine love is hot stuff! If we experienced God head on, our souls would be forced right out of our bodies and our human adventure would be cut off short. That is why scripture says, "No one can see God and live." We are told by those who have had near death experiences that they can't wait to get back there.

FLOWERS *They lose all fear of death.*

KEATING Yes. Here are a few thoughts about how the Trinity works—now that we know these thoughts can only be pointers. It seems to me that the chief purpose of Jesus was to manifest the goodness of the Father and the dispositions that are hidden in the Father's heart. What could these be? Theologians propose that there are three essential relationships in one God; that is, three relationships in one common reality that might be called "the Godhead." The Father enjoys the fullness of the Godhead as source, but source in relationship to the others. The Father is infinite potentiality. The Son is the coming into actuality of all that the Father is. The Father totally gives away to the Son all the riches of the divine nature. The Word of God is the Creator of all that exists. There is no possessiveness in God, no attachment, because he has everything and is everything as its source and sustainer. There is nothing to receive. The Father does not need gifts or service, but gives himself away to more and more creatures insofar as they can receive him.

The Son is the receptive principle in the Trinity, who totally receives the Father. The Son returns himself totally to the Father, and their mutual self-giving is expressed in the Third Person, which is the movement of their common love. This movement is not an aspiration for love and unity, but the sigh of infinite satisfaction and delight in the act of loving, giving, and oneness.

The Son of God becomes flesh, as the Prologue to the Gospel of John proclaims. Now we are in a situation where sacrifice involves suffering, because in the creation of human beings, the Father has communicated to us a significant degree of freedom; hence we can reject him, or pursue our own mad pursuit of happiness through the emotional programs, which can only lead to misery and frustration.

This is how Paul describes the Incarnation: "The Word of God did not consider being God something to cling to, but emptied himself." That is, he totally let go of all the prerogatives of being divine, identified and became one with the lowest form of intelligent beings that we know of, took the lowest place among them, was rejected by the civil and ecclesiastical authorities of his time, and saw his mission shredded before his eyes. What is he doing? He is trying to manifest and communicate what the Father is doing eternally by giving himself to the Son, so that he lives in the Son rather than himself. The Father is eternally emptying himself of everything that he could call his own. Everything in the Trinity is self-giving love, non-possessiveness. Moreover, if Jesus is the true Son of God, he has to manifest the same disposition of total emptying that the Father does in begetting the Son.

The poor, suffering, and dying Jesus is the revelation of the invisible God. We are invited to participate in this immense stream of selfless love.

Everybody, by virtue of being born, is on the spiritual journey. There isn't any other choice. We all have the innate capacity to manifest God because we already are that image by virtue of being created.

The religions of the world have the duty of awakening people to this destiny and of providing the means of acquiring it, such as rituals, sacraments, good deeds, and a deepening relationship with the Ultimate Reality. In Christianity the principal teaching is how to live as human beings in a divine way.

In the Trinity infinite love expresses itself in the total giving away of itself or sacrifice. In becoming a human being, Christ could hardly do less than present a complete and even extreme example of the total gift of himself to the love of the Father. That love is awesome, because it involves, as Paul says, becoming sin for our sake.

FLOWERS *What does "becoming sin" mean?*

KEATING Paul puts it this way "He who knew not sin"—that is, the divine Word—"was made sin." Jesus, in his agony in the garden of Gethsemane, asked to be spared from drinking the cup that symbolized the full human consequences of all the violence, sin, indifference, and horrors of human misbehavior of all of time. If we accept our identity as a human being, we are on the same wavelength as Jesus. We identify with Jesus, as he identified with us.

The descent into hell is the symbol of ultimate identification with the human nature. As one spiritual writer puts it, "Christ, in becoming human, has so taken the lowest place that no one can ever take it from him." In Jesus, love moves to a new level of profundity. Christ was asked to cease to be the beloved of the Father in order to fulfill the Father's will. The greatest love is to give up love for love's sake. So now we are talking about a kind of love that is beyond compassion, or beyond agape—namely, divine love, which is so totally surrendering of itself that there really is nothing left of it. It is utter non-possessiveness, utter freedom. But that is apparently what God is: everything by being no thing.

The movement into the transformative attitudes is a movement of love. Every time we descend to a new level of humility, there, instantly, is a resurrection. The letting go of some part of our false identity enables the Holy Spirit to rush in and give us our true identity, our True Self. In this way, our consciousness becomes not *our* consciousness anymore. Rather, our limited consciousness is perceived to be tucked into the greater consciousness of the Word of God incarnating in us.

I think the most touching thing about the Trinitarian relationships is that all suffering in some way is in God. Nothing of our lives is, in fact, separate from God. As the transforming process unfolds, the details of our lives, motives, choices, and actions are inspired more and more by the divine life that is taking form in us. Our individual personalities, plans, and desires may remain, but without attachment, so that we are free to let them go when circumstances or God take them away. Meanwhile, we need them in some degree in order to live in this world, manifesting in the difficult circumstances of daily life the great mercy and love of God for us and for everyone.

Christian service is not so much what we are doing for others as what Christ *in us* is doing for Christ *in them*. The contemplative journey is the ever-increasing *appreciation* of who God is without fully *knowing* who he is or what he is.

The Ultimate Reality is using everything for the transformation of the human family into the Mystical Body of Christ. Each of us is invited to be a cell in that Body.

Each cell has the whole program of the Mystical Body. The Holy Spirit, like the soul in the body, fills every part and every cell in the body, giving it life. The divine DNA is the Holy Spirit's program for each of us.

Everyone has a vocation in this Body. There is a divine way of being in every vocation, whether it is a garbage man, policeman, mother, or grandma, teacher, sick person, etc., so that ultimately, as Paul puts it, "God is all in all." And this doesn't mean there is nothing else at all, but that there is no proportion between everything else and this vast, boundless, unlimited source of goodness that is the Ground of Being. The process of healing is manifesting what is most important to know, that is, the infinite mercy of God, the one and only possession we really need. We can do without everything else.

FLOWERS *Could you talk a little bit about the Holy Spirit?*

KEATING The Spirit is believed to be the sanctifier since he epitomizes the spirituality of total giving that characterizes the Father and the Son. The word "person" is probably not an adequate term for the relationships within the Trinity, but there are aspects that suggest that Father and Son are appropriate to describe the activities that scripture applies to them. Only the Son of God became flesh. The Spirit flows from the Father and the Son as an expression of their unity.

"The Spirit of the Lord fills the earth is all embracing, and knows man's utterance." The Spirit fills all things and orders all things sweetly. It brings order out of chaos. The Spirit is the source of the whole supernatural organism, the theological virtues, the infused moral virtues, and the Fruits and Gifts of the Holy Spirit. The Spirit is sanctifier, the Paraclete who intercedes for us, the Consoler, and the Advocate who pleads for us.

In my youth the Spirit was called "the forgotten guest." In other words, the Church was so far removed from some of the primary resources of its earlier days that it did not seem to be aware of what the Spirit does, although it was certainly available in the tradition. The externals and legalistic aspects of the Church had so dominated instruction that the most important presence in our lives was virtually unknown. Imagine calling the Holy Spirit "the forgotten guest"! If the most important character in the universe is an unknown, we are in pretty tough shape. This has gradually been replaced, especially with the theology immediately prior, during, and following the Second Vatican Council.

"The love of God is poured forth in our hearts by the Holy Spirit who has been given to us." And "Don't you know that you are the temple of God and that the Spirit dwells within you?" These are texts that reinforce the Divine Indwelling and the fact that when we are silent ourselves, it is in order to be able to listen to the movements and guidance of the Spirit, who dwells in us in such a way as to be the guide and the nurse, so to speak, to teach us divine etiquette, and to transform our dispositions from self-centeredness to the utter generosity of the Divine Host. God has invited us into the banquet of life and still more into the super-banquet of eternal life, which is the food of the divine essence—nourishment designed for the most mature participants in the adventure of human life.

PART EIGHT

Divine Indwelling

FR. KEATING: We are the image of God, and this consists of the grace that communicates to us, through faith, the fact that we are dwelt in by God and that the Trinity lives in us—otherwise known as the "Divine Indwelling." In his farewell discourse at the Last Supper, Jesus speaks of the oneness of our union with God and of the promise of the Father and the Son to come and make their permanent dwelling within us. That God dwells within us as loving Father is affirmed again and again in the Gospel of John.

The Divine Indwelling is the source of profound supernatural powers. The three theological virtues of faith, hope, and charity are part of the endowment of grace and flow organically from the Divine Indwelling. Our natural endowment includes an intellect and will and the interior and exterior senses. The supernatural organism corresponds with these physiological and mental capacities and draws them to a certain integration with our supernatural faculties.

The spiritual journey is therefore not about getting something, but about awakening to the gifts we already have. As a result, our primary response to God's gifts is gratitude and consent—not activity in the form of effort, but rather action in the sense of accepting the goodness of God's presence and unlimited hospitality. As Paul writes, "What have you that you have not received?"

DR. FLOWERS: *But there may be a kind of circularity here for some people who would feel that you already have to have faith to start on this journey to receive faith.*

KEATING: My point is, you already have the image of God within you, with all its potentialities. To lack faith implies an attitude of rejection.

FLOWERS: *That's interesting. So there is a powerful kind of misunderstanding about "the faith journey" here.*

KEATING: In actual fact, we are all standing on our heads, psychologically, and have everything upside down—it is a job to get ourselves right side up. The term "faith" is primarily trust in God. It is not so much an acceptance of propositions as a commitment to surrender to God. Faith is turning one's life over completely to God.

FLOWERS: *And what about hope?*

KEATING: There is a feeling called "hope" that is spontaneous. It is the instinctive reaction to a good that is possible to attain, but not yet present. But the theological virtue of hope is not about that kind of hope. It is not about the future at all. Nor is it about the past. It is rather trust and acceptance of God's infinite mercy right now in the present moment.

Infinite mercy is not based on anything we've done or not done, but is simply part of the sheer gratuity of grace, in which God is prepared to forget all our negative behavior in the past and would prefer that we entrust ourselves entirely to him and not think about it either. So it is a movement into the present moment.

This kind of hope is not based on how good you may have been or how evil you may have been, but about who you are now. If at this moment your will is turned over to God, you are exercising the infused virtue of hope. "And hope is not disappointed but the love of God is poured forth in our hearts by the Holy Spirit that has been given to us."

Hope liberates us from the whole burden of the past. It is not based on anything temporary or illusory, but on the very nature of God, which is infinite mercy, power, and goodness. Our virtues mean nothing, and our sins are no longer obstacles. We are now completely with God in the present moment, whatever God wants that to be. The habitual exercise of hope is an enormous liberation from beating ourselves to death for past misdemeanors, real or imaginary, and from the endless sifting through our motives for past actions that we can never quite recapture. To forget self by giving it to God is the direction that hope invites us to take.

Charity is the growth of selfless love, which is the life of the Trinity. The stream of charity comes forth from the Father, flows into the Son, and comes to its quintessence in the spirituality of the Holy Spirit. The stream of charity is circulating in the Trinity all the time, as a kind of river—something more dynamic than just a stream. It is an ocean of love into which we are invited to participate and are gradually lured into that endless circular motion of receiving, passing on, and giving back. Jesus expresses his experience of it this way: "I came forth from the Father and have come into the world and now I leave the world and return to the Father."

All creation has come forth from the Father and remains in the Father as its Source. God manifests himself in the most material and gross forms of creation. Evolution is the return of everything to the Source, bringing with it all of creation, each according to its capacity or nature, so that everything created may rest in the bosom of the Father and participate in the divine nature.

Charity involves assimilating the same dispositions towards creation as are present in the Trinity, mainly, unconditional love; then the willingness to forgive everything and anything; interior freedom from compulsion; forgetfulness of ourselves and detachment from over-identifying with our body, thoughts, and feelings – in short, recognizing the difference between our mind and our True Self. The theological virtues gradually transform our intellects and wills into the mind and heart of God.

Then there are the "Fruits of the Spirit" listed in Galatians 5:22, which are specific terms for the spontaneous acts of the Spirit expressing the theological virtues both during prayer and in practical contact with daily life. Charity, joy, and peace are the first three. Joy is not so much exuberance, but the sense of well-being and a positive attitude towards life in spite of difficulties, tragedies, and pain.

Peace, in the classical definition, is the tranquility of order. It means that one is not compulsively inclined to one or other attitude towards the different moral issues that arise in everyday life. Thus it avoids extremes. Every virtue has its opposite. Moderation is a manifestation of prudence, balance, and spiritual poise with regard to the diverse activities of everyday life.

Goodness is perceiving the presence of God in everything, especially in nature and in other people. This gift was prominent in Mother Teresa whose faith, perfected by this fruit, saw Christ in the poor and the destitute people that she picked up off the streets of Calcutta.

> **FLOWERS:** *That is why she never lost her energy to do that work. She was always embracing her Beloved. So the work fed her.*

KEATING: Without that gift, she could see only the ugliness and repulsiveness and feel the desire to pass by that characterizes a merely human reaction to destitution.

> **FLOWERS:** *If we serve, we serve out of a sense of obligation. And then sometimes it's a burden on the spirit of the one we're serving.*

KEATING: Yes, it can be a form of domination.

> **FLOWERS:** *And a kind of dutifulness. But when Mother Teresa held those lepers, it was more like a love feast.*

KEATING: Because what she was seeing was not what we ordinarily see with the bodily eyes. She saw with the inner eye of faith raised to penetrating insight by this special fruit of the Spirit. The qualities infused into our hearts and freely given by God lead to transformation. With these gifts, we are more than qualified for transformation in Christ. To continue describing these Fruits of the Spirit—faithfulness is the tireless fidelity to our commitments, no matter what happens. Patience is an attitude of waiting for God, or for the resolution of dilemmas, problems, and difficulties for any length of time and as long as God wills. It strengthens the infused moral virtue of fortitude, which is to persevere in seeking the difficult good, no matter how hard the circumstances may be. It is a virtue that is especially important for perseverance in our relationships and commitment to the spiritual journey.

The Fruits of the Spirit are not obtrusive. They may pass unnoticed by others because they are not that striking or sensational. They gradually increase our sensitivity to the presence of God, and as that overall presence increases, so do they. All this while, one is absorbing the mind and heart of Christ. In other words, as a cell in the Body of Christ, one is beginning to express the divine DNA in one's own particular location in the Body. The supernatural organism is the presence and the exercise of the risen life of Christ in us. So, in a sense, the greatest proof of Christ's Resurrection is his action within us manifested through the infused virtues and Fruits and Gifts of the Spirit and the Beatitudes that flow from them.

FLOWERS: *It has always struck me that the only promise that God repeatedly makes in scripture is to be present. He doesn't promise that we won't suffer, he doesn't promise that we won't be hungry, but, "I will be with you." That's his one promise, always.*

KEATING: Yes. He never said the spiritual journey was a magic carpet to bliss. His exhortation to "Come follow me" suggests not only following him down the dusty roads of Galilee, but to the cross. But let's not stop at his death, or even his descent into hell. To follow Christ is to go to all those spiritual places or states of consciousness that he endured, and then to share his Resurrection and his Ascension, which is his return to the bosom of the Father. Such is the full development of the Resurrection.

As St. Paul dares to say, all of us cells in the Mystical Body are already present with Christ at the right hand of the Father. The head of the body is already there, so we are gradually catching up with our Source. The Ascension is the ultimate manifestation of the resurrected life in us. It is the capacity to see Christ active and triumphing over suffering and the apparent destruction of all goodness and the descent of human behavior into worse and worse situations.

In all of these, there remains hidden the light of the Resurrection and the power of the Ascension.

The Fruits of the Spirit, as profound as they are in bringing the theological virtues to their full stature, are surpassed by the still greater and more profound seven-fold Gifts of the Spirit, enumerated in Isaiah 11:2 and applied in St. Matthew's Gospel in the Beatitudes.

"Blessed" means something like "congratulations." It is a complete reversal of human values and totally counter-cultural. The Beatitudes are Jesus' idea of happiness as well as his own experience. No one was ever poorer than he in the sense that he gave up the treasures of divinity to become incarnate and even more so in his passion and death. The divine essence is the supreme value, and that is what he surrendered. To use Paul's words, "He did not consider being equal to God something to cling to." Jesus refers to this disposition in the Beatitude: "Blessed are the pure of heart for they shall see God." This Beatitude refers to perfect humility.

The Fruit of the Spirit called "goodness" sees God in everything; the Beatitude of purity of heart is to see everything in God. To see God in everything and everything in God is to see nothing but God. This points to the sublime and transforming meaning of such phrases in Paul as "Christ will be everything in everyone." Or, "God will be all in all.

PART NINE

Divine
Transformation

DR. FLOWERS *Jesus talks about "the inner room." I'd like to know what goes on in that inner room.*

FR. KEATING If you remember, it is in the context of prayer that Jesus speaks of the inner room. He starts by saying, "If you want to pray"—implying that if you want a relationship with God, or a deeper one than you now have, this formula might be helpful. This formula is the basis for the Centering Prayer practice, which is a contemporary way of carrying it out.

In the inner room, two things are taking place. One is the affirmation of our basic goodness. God affirms the fact that we have been created in his image and likeness. He does so by a variety of affirmative experiences, such as a sense of peace, or that everything is okay, or that God loves us.

The second is the purification of the unconscious. This includes the unloading of the repressed emotional material from early childhood that needs to be evacuated by coming to consciousness again or for the first time, and experiencing the feelings that we had repressed. It also includes our unconscious over-identification with our group, whether that is family, clan, village, tribe, country, city-state, religion, ethnic group, peer group, gang, or, nowadays, the global village.

FLOWERS *Do you think it would be possible to over-identify with the global village?*

KEATING The false self is capable of over-identifying with anything at all. So to prevent it from doing so, the Divine Therapy invites us to accept the purification of the unconscious, including the depth of the unconscious that can't normally be reached by a simple reflective process, but that requires the special action of divine love. This deep love casts a penetrating light that reveals over time whatever is hidden in our unconscious. The residue of the false self is still embedded in the unconscious even after the transforming effects of the Fruits and Gifts of the Spirit have begun to appear.

Whether it can be entirely corrected in this life is hard to say. But as far as I can see, the divine action keeps searching and healing as long as one lives. The emotional programs for happiness are embedded in who we think we are and who we want to become in order to be happy. The purification of the unconscious heals the pride, aggressiveness, and self-centeredness of the false self at its roots.

One of the Seven Gifts of the Holy Spirit, specifically the Gift of Knowledge, addresses the whole area of attachment to the emotional programs for happiness by communicating to us intuitively the conviction that only God can satisfy our boundless desire for happiness. The withdrawal of the affirmations and consolations we enjoyed in our previous relationship with God is the necessary remedy for our over-attachment to those emotional programs and to the groups with which we excessively identify ourselves. We may interpret this development as a loss of God's friendship, which may put us into a grieving process.

It is not enough just to do Centering Prayer itself, even if this is done twice a day. At the same time one must carry into daily life the effects of the practice. So there is a balance of the activities that are going on in the inner room. One must not neglect either aspect of the Divine Therapy. Daily life challenges our attitudes and actively brings to consciousness, through events, what is passively brought to consciousness in the purification of the unconscious during Centering Prayer. Life in community can bring to our attention aspects of the dark side of our personality that silence and solitude alone might not be able to do.

FLOWERS *That makes it sound as if other people we find difficult are also helpful in our path by bringing us up against the things that need to be purified on the personal, unconscious level.*

KEATING Yes. Our enemies or those who rub us the wrong way are telling us something about ourselves. It doesn't necessarily mean there is anything wrong with them.

FLOWERS *Forgive them, for they know not how much they are helping us!*

KEATING We often project onto others what we most dislike in ourselves. This is why bringing our prayer life into confrontation with the reality of daily life, with its unexpected happenings and ups and downs, is a very important part of the purification and transformative process and has been called "the discipline of the Holy Spirit."

FLOWERS *So even if you wanted to, it's not a good idea, and not effective, to stay in the inner room all the time?*

KEATING The founder of the Benedictine tradition, St. Benedict, legislated that newcomers should not be allowed to live as hermits, but should subject themselves to community life for many years before undertaking the solitude of the desert, which has specific problems. The fourth-century Desert Fathers, who experimented with all forms of monastic life, both in community and in total solitude, discovered that the false self was equally active in complete solitude as in the wear and tear of life in community. They found themselves getting just as angry at trifles there as they did when they experienced the faults of the brethren in the cenobium, some of which were aggravating and sometimes even unbearable. Others are not usually the problem, but an invitation to look into our own motivation and mindsets. What is it in me that makes this person or this situation seem so distressing?

As time goes on, the Divine Therapist extends the walls of the inner room to the whole of life so that everything becomes a part of the process of liberation and empowerment. Having faced the dark side of our personality through the intimate experience of self-centeredness in all its forms, the divine action then tends to focus on our over-identification with our roles, thoughts, feelings, bodies, and even our self-identity.

As Jesus put it, "unless you deny your inmost self you cannot be my disciple."

All serve to work comprehensively with the Divine Therapy that we are receiving in the inner room, bringing us to the point where we can unload all the material that we had repressed and can then move on to the purification of love, which addresses our attachments to groups that we belong to and invites us to move beyond our dependence on them for our self-identity.

Prayer in secret is the forgetfulness of self. If thoughts of self-reflection arise—"How am I doing?" or, "Is this the prayer of quiet?"—we can recognize that this is just the ego. Any reflection on self in prayer is the ego. As that conviction deepens, it becomes easier to say goodbye to the habitual movements of the false self.

The pervasive, non-possessive attitude towards ourselves is the awakening of the Kingdom of God in us, or Christ-consciousness. Now the purification of the unconscious and development of the supernatural organism into Christ consciousness coincide, and transformation then unfolds. Each process, in its own way, leads to the manifestation of true humility and pure love. The two processes are probably the same, or at least two sides of the same coin. There is now no place to go since you are already there. But you didn't get there on your own steam. To be there without getting there is the epitome of the transformative process.

The True Self is who we really are as manifestations of God, but is more or less unknown to us, or buried in the unconscious because of the development of our false self.

Beyond the True Self is the Ultimate Self, or the deepest self, which is God, or in Christian terminology, "Christ in us." As Paul puts it, "I live now not I, but Christ lives in me." The theologian Raimon Panikkar adds, "… lives in me as my deepest self."

So we could almost translate that in the light of Paul's very strong statement, "I live not I, but Christ lives in me." Perhaps we could even say, "I live now not I, but Christ *is* me." This would not be unknown in Christian tradition. As Catherine of Genoa put it in medieval Italy, "There is no me but God." On the other hand, we can never totally rid ourselves of the fact that we are created and have a separate self and a uniqueness that can never be repeated.

To be really real, I have to allow my identity to be changed and placed at the disposal of the Divine Will, so that my spiritual will is totally in union with God's will. John of the Cross taught that the state of transformation in Christ is the transformation of our intellect and will into the divine intellect and will. There is then no movement in us except under the influence of the Holy Spirit, and all our actions are emerging from an abiding disposition of surrender, silence, and receptivity that is the complete integration of contemplative prayer and action.

The assimilation of the mind of Christ is what the transformative process is and what it looks like when it's completed. The exercise of the Fruits and Gifts of the Spirit are signs of the True Self and reveal the image of God in us.

If we could just relax into who we actually are—Christ in us, at the ultimate level—we would understand what the Fathers of the Church meant by "deification," or "transformation in Christ." This is the divine plan for us both as individuals and as the human family have.

PRESS & MAGAZINE

At Wayfarer Books we believe poetry is the language of the earth. We believe words, like rivers through wild places, can change the shape of the world. We publish poets and writers and renegades who stand outside of mainstream culture; poets, essayists, and storytellers whose work might withstand the scrutiny of crows and coyotes, those who are cryptic and floral, the crepuscular, and the queer-at-heart. We are more than just a publisher but a community of writers. Our mission is to produce books that can serve as a compass and map to all wayfarers through wild terrain.

WAYFARERBOOKS.ORG

SUPPORTING INDIGENOUS FUTURES
1% GIVEN BACK

Wayfarer Books is based in the San Juan Mountains near Mesa Verde, on the lands of the Ancestral Pueblo, the Southern Ute, the Weenuche (Mountain Ute), the Diné (Navajo), and the San Juan Southern Paiute Tribe. We honor the generations of Indigenous communities who have stewarded these lands for thousands of years. We acknowledge that this place was taken through genocide, colonization, and displacement. We respect the Indigenous peoples who remain here, both past and present. As one concrete act of accountability, we are launching 1% Given Back. Beginning in 2026, we will give 1% of Wayfarer's net profits directly to the Indigenous nations on whose lands we are based, in support of sovereignty, Indigenous futures, and wealth redistribution. We do this in the belief that acknowledgment should move beyond words and into tangible practice.

LEARN MORE AT WAYFARERBOOKS.ORG